Advance _ _ _ _ _

"I love the voice in these poems, so accessible, so conversational, yet frequently able to extract from the ordinary places and everyday moments of our lives a kind of holy instant, of joy, of tenderness, of wonder, of insight that is 'crisp as snapped fingers.' Eric Nelson's poems are peopled with chickens, guns and lovers, poets and writers, mountains and dogwoods and camellias, and lots of birds. Plus more than a couple of dogs. And his poems have something of the genius of dogs about them, knowing when and exactly how to roll around in dead and earthy things, and consistently sniffing out the 'loamy aroma of love.'"

—Paul Hostovsky, author of *The Bad Guys* and *Selected Poems*

"In his powerful new collection, *Some Wonder*, Eric Nelson takes his reader 'abroad' (and beyond) in the most refined sense of those directives. He takes us deeply into experience and into the uniqueness of place. The language is lucid, lyrical, and exactly narrative. Yet the mystery of small moments is everywhere present: in each stanza, every poem. We observe the subtle nature of the draft lottery—as each number is drawn, death is delivered to young men. Like a maimed baby, it is born. And these newly assigned soldiers will indeed march as gray numerals into Viet Nam's muck and murder. We feel the rage of the blind professor as he trips over a desk, and we viscerally encounter dead twins on the bottom of a pool holding hands. A striking but ordinary union... as one human reaches out in desperation for another. Eric Nelson listens for the world. He sees and brings

home the delicately dark amazement of being alive as "…
the small ugly god overlook[s] the world it brought to
our senses." God here is a hideous but prophetic frog.
Nelson's poetic sensibility, this collection as a whole
binds the reader to its heart. Page by page, we travel to
inward places of profound depth. And exterior locales
that were always there but never quite seen in such a
surgical and carefully lit manner. Let us 'remain within
ourselves,' that sanctuary we alone occupy, as we sit to
read this quite marvelous collection of poems: *Some
Wonder* by a master poet."
> —Katherine Soniat, author of *The Swing Girl*
> and *Bright Stranger*

"Reading these new poems by Eric Nelson, some
may wonder that his work is not more widely known.
Interweaving fertility and mortality, the poems brim with
a reverential incredulity. With its signature tenderness
for human vulnerability, an expansive sense of place, and
crystalline language threaded with wit, *Some Wonder* is a
collection that appeals on every page."
> —A. E. Stringer, author of *Late Breaking* and
> *Human Costume*

"The wonders of this superb book begin with its
clear, graceful, and accessible language. Yes, *Some Wonder*
is certainly a book you can give with confidence to your
friend who 'doesn't get poetry.' But it's much more than
that. Eric Nelson is a consummate practitioner of the art
that hides art; his plainspoken poems are artful indeed
in their lyrical music, apt metaphors, and strikingly vivid
images. His vision is mature, intelligent, honest, and
subtle. Whether writing about backyard chickens, dead
friends, bodily odors, dog walking, punctuation marks,
or the ordinary joys and sorrows of family life, Nelson

shows that there is nothing more wondrous, finally, than ordinary life passing through the lens of a rich imagination."

—David Graham, author of *Second Wind* and *Magic Shows*

"Eric Nelson is a barker in a language bazaar, and *Some Wonder* is, well, some wonder of lyric and imagistic intensity. Nelson creates striking worlds in his poetry, torturous and depraved and lovely worlds that challenge and seduce. *Some Wonder* is fearsome writing, and Nelson plumbs the deep waters of our best and worst dreams—from twins as they drown at the bottom of a pool, holding hands as 'they drifted as they had in amniotic water/where death and love are the same,' to images of drought, where 'a cardinal redder than fire/bathes in the dust.' *Some Wonder* is filled with poems that take risks, 'like a circus tent in flames,' where we 'begin to look for the alarm we missed.' Don't miss reading this terrific book of poems."

— Seth Brady Tucker, judge and author of *We Deserve the Gods We Ask For*

Also by Eric Nelson

The Twins
Terrestrials
The Interpretation of Waking Life
The Light Bringers
On Call

SOME WONDER

Poems

by Eric Nelson

Winner of the Gival Press Poetry Award

Arlington, Virginia

Published by Gival Press, an imprint of Gival Press, LLC.

For information please write:
Gival Press, LLC
P. O. Box 3812
Arlington, VA 22203
www.givalpress.com

First edition

ISBN: 978-1-940724-02-7
eISBN: 978-1-940724-03-4
Library of Congress Control Number: 2015942115

Cover art © Underworld | Dreamstime.com – Hat on the Road

Book Design by Ken Schellenberg.

My thanks to the editors of the magazines and anthologies in which these poems were previously published:

About Place: "Dogwoods in October"
Arts & Letters Prime: "Men," "The Fence Line," "The Body Smells"
Cincinnati Review: "I Love Chickens"
Clapboard House: "In Another Year"
Comstock Review: "The Yard in April," "The Tenderness of Ice"
Dog Blessings: "Good Dog"
Heron Tree: "Drought"
Lake Effect: "A Small Hole"
The McNeese Review: "Our Wars"
New Madrid: "The Lowcountry"
New Ohio Review: "Gun on the Table," "The Egg"
Other Voices International: "Guitars," "Feeders"
The Oxford American: "Small Ugly God"
Poetry: "Apostrophe to the Apostrophe"
Poetry East: "Picture Day"
Prime Number: "Thanksgiving Matinee"
Snakeskin: "Visiting Writer"
Southern Poetry Review: "The System," "December 19th," "Old Glasses"
Stone, River, Sky: "Georgia Sunset"
The Southern Poetry Anthology: "The Lowcountry," "Fair Road," "In Another Year"
The Southern Review: "The Rose Bus"
The Sun: "The Twins," "Twenty-five O'Clock," "Better Angels"

Three Line Poetry: "Small Wonders" (sections 1, 4, 8, 10, 12)

Valparaiso Review: "In Her Memory"

"Professor Cook" won the 2013 Porter Fleming Poetry Prize

"Wheelchair on the Beach" won the 2014 Bettie Sellers Poetry Award

"The Rose Bus," "The Twins," and "In Her Memory" appeared in the chapbook, *The Twins*, published by Split Oak Press, 2009

"At the bottom of the hill was MacSheen's Store where Grandmother Caron bought me red sodas. The store was carried off behind us. The world itself was water sliding around us."
— from *Fishing, With What I Have* – PC

Contents

The System

My son, age four, appears
Beside the bed, middle of the night
Whispering in my ear
That the neighbor's system is on.
Though he can't tell time, he says
They're watering the yard
At one in the morning.
I'm still surfacing from sleep
But remember this week, seeing
The lawn backhoed, leveled, networked
With pipes, timers, pressure monitors,
Then completely re-sodded, the entire
System an extravagant waste.
I walk Ben back to his room and we stand
At his window hypnotized
By a watery chapel all silver and mist
Created by dozens of arching, overlapping
Sprays, the only sound in the star-still night
The shh-shh-shh of the sprinklers.

Drought

The clouds' lies are unforgivable.
Lake gone, canoe aground,
Nothing but cracked beds.
For once everyone knows exactly
What they want. I remember
A sound above me, pattering,
Like kisses, but sincere, rivering
Down the window, hanging
Like bells from the bird feeder.
The alarm chimes in the dark.
I rise and run ahead of the sun.
Outside the treatment center
The addicts are already waiting,
Smoking and pacing, grass
Crackling beneath them.
From somebody's pocket
A phone wails like a siren
Everyone pretends not to hear.
A cardinal redder than fire
Bathes in the dust.

The Twins

The five-year-old twins who wandered
From their yard were finally found

Side by side in their matching suits
On the bottom of a neighbor's pool

Staring at the sky through six feet
Of inviting water, holding hands.

On the roster of horrors, theirs is not
The worst, not even close. Children die

Every day and often more than one
In the same family, as in the car wreck

Yesterday that killed four boys, two of them
Brothers, driving to play a basketball game.

Or when Santa arrived at the Christmas
Party and gunned down his own family.

Yet years after it happened I still
Think of the twins, their fathomless

Panic, the froth of their flailing.
And then the moment they stopped

Trying to live, grasped each other's hand
And let go—the way strangers took hands

And let go of the melting towers.
Their separate struggles pressed

Flat between their clasped palms,
Neither of them afraid alone,

They drifted as they had in amniotic water
Where death and love are the same.

Picture Day

All morning, under warning, they stayed
Unstained, pressed and brushed, waiting
For their moment to be petrified.
The posing over, hungry and free
They swarm the lunchroom
With clacking trays, unwrapping
Themselves, spilling soup and milk,
Talking with their mouths full of missing teeth.

The photographer, all coos and chuckles
Earlier, lugs his equipment out the door.
The children settle into steady eating
And murmuring, ignoring the sobs
Of the boy in the middle of the row
Staring at his tray, his tears dripping.
He always cries, every day, cried
As his picture was made.
A teacher rubs his back, whispers to him
And reminds the others not to pass
The napkins they know
He will shred and scatter like feathers.

When the bell rings they rise, awkward
As baby birds—hair wild, ribbons undone,
Shirts unfurled and wrinkled
As the brown bags they drop into the trash
Before they sleep-walk, single-file, to their rooms.
Only the one who weeps remains
Unchanged—his white shirt still stiff,
Black pants still creased, hair in place.

Men

During the party that promised
To rage long into the night
The baby in the upstairs room woke up
And cried relentlessly. Finally

The baby's young father took him
To the back of the back yard and stood
In the quiet cradling him, whispering,
Swaying slightly from side to side.

One at a time four or five of his friends
Came looking for him.
They stood in a circle swaying, saying
Nothing, all of them still swaying

Long after the baby fell asleep,
The light and music and laughter
From the house not quite reaching them.

Wheelchair on the Beach

An old woman in a wheelchair is pushed
Toward the ocean by a middle-aged woman.
It's slow going—the sand soft, the wheels
Bogging down, not turning. Red-faced,
She shoves, strains, digs
Her feet into the hot sand to inch
The chair forward, sliding more than rolling it.
The old woman, wrapped in a white robe,
Clutches the dark blanket in her lap.
Her hair is a small white cloud, her face
Sharp and fiery.
Carrying my cooler
And umbrella, heading for the parking lot,
I'm embarrassed to be staring, staring
Anyway, torn between admiring
Their resolve and hating their foolishness.
Who could think this was a good idea—
The old woman yearning to touch the ocean
One last time, feel salt on her papery skin,
Or the younger one, daughter
I decide, wanting something meaningful
To remember?
I drive home remembering
The chair mired in damp sand, the old woman
Facing the waves rolling toward her,
Her daughter—the chair handles holding her up—
Leaning over, her head touching her mother's,
Her body swelling to catch its breath.

December 19th

After the call that rang me out of sleep
Into my mother's death, I stepped outside
And watched the white sun rise
Behind a mesh of fogged-in evergreens.

I turned off the dripping faucets.
Pushed back the stiffened sheets
I had draped across the camellias.
Shivering in my robe I looked across the street
At my neighbor's twinkling Christmas tree.

My mother scoffed at talk of life beyond.
This life was the only one she believed.
But as I stared I swear I heard her speak
As firmly as she did when I was young.
Son, she said, *go inside before you freeze.*

Our Wars

He was a nerd before there were nerds
But one thing you had to say for Mark—
The guy knew how to die. In our wars
He was the first to scream *I'm hit*, tumble,
Sprawl, pitch forward face first, call
Mama and go still, not flinching
The gnats from his eyes
Because this was death and he knew
The physics—body in motion, opposite
And equal—wherever it takes you.
We envied him, we who were afraid to risk
A rash, a tear, our mothers' wrath.
He perfected the staggering collapse,
The high-speed-tree-collide-and-ricochet,
The twirl-into-prickly-vines.
D-Day at the beach, knee-deep in surf, we'd barely
Begun when Mark screamed, clasped his head
And fell into the dead man's float. The rest of us
Zig-zagged through sound effects—burping guns,
Whistling missiles—until we made it up the beach
To the picnic table, bellowed triumph, took slugs
From canteens and ran toward the smoking grill.
When Mark staggered up dripping, he wanted
To know why we hadn't waited for him, if we knew
How long he'd held his breath. We didn't look at him—
Nobody told him to die. We planned another assault.

Blackout

Boredom, weed, testosterone—
Who knows why
Aimless nights in the car
Listening to music
One of us could yell
Blackout and the driver had to kill
The headlights, pitching us
Into the rush of hurling
Forward blind, screaming
For as long as the driver's nerve held out.

* * * * *

Our year of the Draft, a month
After high-school ended
We watched the Lottery
Like we were watching a game—
Hyped and smart-assed, chips
And cokes on my parents' coffee table.
Screw the draft and Vietnam.
Screw Uncle Ho and Uncle Sam.

A gray old man began to draw, slowly, one
By one, 365 capsules from a glass drum,
Three of them carrying our birth dates,
The rest no concern of ours.
Before we were settled, still jostling
For the popcorn and recliner,
The gray man pulled up Joe's date
And announced it like a bingo number.
We looked at each other to be sure
We'd heard what we heard. We looked
Until Joe kicked the table and slammed outside,
Coke cans bouncing like hand grenades.

Ronnie and I turned back to the screen
And watched closely, wanting both
For this to end and for it to go on—
The longer the safer.

One after another the dates were drawn,
Declared, delivered
To the giant board in the background.

Ronnie's birthday came up in the hundreds,
High enough not to worry
Unless the war got worse.
And mine, December 10, was number 362.

****

Joe started lifting weights and grew
Gung-ho, eager to kill gooks.
Ronnie faded into church missions.
I read every book
On the recommended list,
Training for college.

Before summer ended and we lost
Each other for good, we drove a few times more,
Blasting Hendrix, the Doors, Big Brother
From one back road to another.
Staring at the small pool the headlights spilled
Ahead of us, we listened, sang along, waited
Until it was clear to all of us that no one
Would be the first to shout *Blackout.*

Professor Cook

1.

He was football player big, wore a suit
Every class and carried a black satchel
Thick with notebooks written in braille.
His eyes fixed in a permanent squint,
He stared at the back wall and called roll,
Fingering each figure of our names
As if he knew us like no one else did,
Not even us, as if he meant to strum
A chord inside us—a call as textured
As our names—rippling outward
Until we meant it when we answered *Here.*
When he finished attendance he began
To lecture, monotonously, his hands
Still, his squinting eyes aimed above our heads.

2.

He liked to shake us up by looking out
The window and making a comment—
Looks like rain he might say, or *I love the wind.*
He didn't expect us to speak, but once,
Striding into the classroom he smashed hard
Into an out-of-place desk, yelped shrilly
And dropped his satchel. For the first time
He looked blind, uncertain, jerky, groping
The desk until he pulled himself upright
And spoke in controlled but unconcealed rage,

Why didn't you move that desk? What the hell
Is wrong with you? Nobody spoke. Nobody
Looked when he called the roll, but we felt him
Pressing every letter of our stupid names.

Visiting Writer

I'm tired of your face
Appearing before me, smiling,
Your fullback's body in professor clothes—
Sport coat and chinos and worn satchel,
Black leather as supple as your sentences.
I'm ready to tuck you away to bring out
When I want to, when I'm ready. Like a book.

But you keep popping up uninvited, unscheduled.
Every day. In a student's mouth. In a feral cat
Outside my window. In the parking lot I circle.
Beside me in the car driving to the airport
To pick up visiting writers. I'm tired of them
Coming and going, coming and going
So rapidly I remember only their luggage.
I'm moving forward but it feels like swimming
Backstroke at night in a pool with no walls.

Today it was 10:15 before you showed. Late.
You were never late. I was going
Over my notes when I looked up
To see you standing at the lectern
Introducing the visiting writer. All that time,
None of us knew you were the one visiting.
One day the day will go by without you.
Then another. Then the visits will end,
The work remain.

Dogwoods In October

Who doesn't love them in spring when they're all
Foam and prance, bright enough to make you wince,
Majorettes of the March parade? But now—

Saggy, liver-spotted, leaves more rust than red, dozing
Through the maples' fiery strip, not sap enough
For even one last fling—who notices now?

Casketed in drab foliage, invisible
To the uncorrected eye, siren-red berries—round
As peepholes—offer glimpses of the other side.

In Her Memory

Ten months after she came through town
On a visiting writer gig and you fell in love
With her as you fell for every smart, gifted,
Lovely woman you met, I ran into her
And her husband at a conference and at first
She didn't remember me, which was no surprise—
How long was she here, a day-and-a-half?
But then she did, I think, and we chatted
Superficially while I remembered
The little current that jumped between the two of you,
An uplift in your voices when you spoke to each other
At dinner that night, the extra clink of your wine
Glasses when you toasted her reading, visit, presence.
Oh she was charmed because you were charming
In the way you always were — and then some.
My guess is that you kept in touch with her
As you did with so many people you met and admired,
Sending them compliments, poems, your heart.
As we chatted in the hotel lobby I thought
I should tell her that you are dead, killed
Three months after she was here, and as soon
As I thought it I knew that I couldn't
Stand to see her face suddenly alter
With the force of it, her whole body sag as if a few
Small bones were abruptly pulled out of her.
I couldn't stand to explain what happened or say
I don't know to so many of her questions.
I realized the enormous control I had—
The power to change her entirely in an instant
Or let her remain as alive as you are
In her memory, and I took selfish comfort in that,

Stirring it with the guilt I felt for not telling her.
I don't recall a single thing we said to each other but soon
She was walking off with her husband happy
She said to have seen me again and maybe, as I slid
Into the revolving door, she remembered you
With a little smile still alive.

A Small Hole

First was the whispering above us in our sleep.
Not every night. Intermittently. Unpredictably
It woke us and we listened, trying to understand.
When we touched the ceiling, it stopped—listened
To us listening—waited. We vowed to know it
But by daylight we thought better to live
And let live, get to work, soon enough it will end.
Then the ragged hole appeared above our bed.
We bandaged it like an ear with packing tape.
The whispering continued, widened the hole.
I climbed with poison into the attic's beams
And struts and gently set the tray. In days
The rank rot began seeping down into the house.
We burned candles and incense but it wouldn't be
    hidden.
We bathed in it. Ate in it. Made love. Imagined its mouth
Moving over us. Then the flies arrived, climbing the
    walls,
Washing their feet in the folds of the curtains, dimming
    the lights
Where they gathered, humming their one-note hymn.

In Another Year

All your students will be gone.
No one dropping your name in class,
Reciting you from memory.
None of your bits in their mouths.
The first year after you died it seemed
Entire classes were yours and I
Was the substitute asking where the chalk is.
The next year they thinned but I knew
Them by their moves, their sudden lunge
For the jugular. Now just a few remain and mostly
I discover them by chance, like after class
Last week when I saw a sheet on a desk
And thought it was the definitions
I'd just distributed, but it turned out to be
That Jack Gilbert poem you always taught.
In another year the building will be filled
With students who know you
As a scholarship fund, not you in the world
You insisted they witness—including you
In your yellowing body those final weeks.
Whenever they wanted explanation
You told them instead to observe
How the man shifts repeatedly the weight
Of the heavy box so that he never
Collapses, but can never put it down.
I don't know if it is grief renewed or
Relief when I see your students disappearing.
I only know that today a dark spear
Streaked toward me on the sidewalk then
Passed through my body like I wasn't there
And when I looked up I had to shield my eyes
To see a hawk pass between me and the sun.

Thanksgiving Matinee

On a day that feels like thanks for nothing
I'm unexpectedly grateful for the shadowy
Woman in the darkened theater walking
Down the incline—one hand full of popcorn,
One full of giant cup—peering side to side.

Adjusted to the dark, I ignore the trailers
Loaded with explosions, chases, guns
To watch her, suspense building, pulling
For her to find who she's looking for.
When she knows she's gone too far she starts
Back up the slope, scanning, pausing,

Until finally she picks up speed and enters
The row I'm in, nothing between us but empty seats.
Soon she is lowering herself into the seat beside me
Whispering *God, I thought I'd never find you.*
And, like her, for an instant I believe she has.

The Egg

We're sitting at the table the way people do
When a family member dies and a stream of well-wishers
Arrive with sympathy and food.

Everyone is concerned for the widow, 70, tough, wiry,
Who now seems weak and befuddled, staring at people
She's known for years without answering,

Rising and walking out the back door, staring at the woods
At the far end of their land.
Returning to the table without a word.

We're all thinking how often one spouse dies
Soon after the other, dies of nothing
But lack. Because we are surrounded by guns, her husband's

Sizeable collection—pistols in glass cases, rifles
In racks and corners—talk turns to their value, the merits
Of revolvers versus semi–autos, plinking, protection.

Now, for the first time, the widow speaks, remembering
That she went to the coop this morning and found curled
In a nesting box a snake, unhinged mouth filled

With a whole egg, disappearing a swallow at a time.
She walked back to the house, pulled her .410
Off the rack, returned to the coop and blew its head off.

A hog-nose, she says. *A good snake. But I had to.*
She shrugs her shoulders. *I had to.* Glancing
At each other, relieved, we nod in agreement.

Better Angels

Adrift, unpinned, their lost feathers
Settle at my feet. Heads cocked,
Clucking, the chickens follow me
Listening to my prayers
Which are plans for the garden—
Fig trees, blueberries, a bridge
Across a pond crackling
With flame-bright fish.
I can't abide angels, overrated
Guardians of no one.
I believe in these earthy
Murmurers patrolling
My yard in plain attire,
Keeping their wings to
Themselves, flying only
In emergencies, gracelessly
And close to the ground—
Where emergencies occur.

Twenty-Five O'clock

In this saved hour I want to praise
The otherworldly feel of it—
As if physics and gravity were a phase
Outgrown and now, at last, what we suspected
Was possible is possible, the future behind us.
In this gifted time it's fine to talk about the slow
Moon hanging in a tree like a paper lantern,
Air crisp as snapped fingers. Whatever comes next
Makes sense, like sleeping on the ocean, nothing
Sounder or stranger than water holding you up.
This hour is not extra loneliness, more reasons to die.
Not another love lost to the brutal swamp.
The world is not too good for us nor we for it.
A saxophone and a woman's laughter flirt
In a window high above the street, the day pulling
Gray blankets to its chin. This bestowed hour
I speak a language I don't understand, repeat
The magic word death without flinching. The hole
In my sleeve disappears. And everything up it.
Some wonder what I mean. Some wonder is what.

Apostrophe to the Apostrophe

Small floater, you stay above the fray,
A wink at nothing's nod, a raised brow
Watching p's and q's, a selfless mote
Between I and·m, little horn of plenty
Spilling plurals, disdaining the bottom line.

Unlike your twin relatives—groupies of wit
And wisdom, hangers on in the smallest talk—
You work alone, dark of a crescent moon.
Laboring in obscurity, you never ask why,
Never exclaim, never tell anyone where to go.

Caught up between extremes, you are both
A turning away and a stepping forth,
A loss and an addition. You are the urge
To possess everything, and the sure sign
That something is missing.

Small Ugly God

To the untended water-garden
By our back steps a frog has come.
For a time we knew it only by a splash
When we opened the door, splash
And tremble of the horse tails and umbrella grass.

Then, sometimes, if we kept still we'd spot
Between the green mesh its dark, volcanic back
Jutting from the water and its eyes—black holes
Drawing us in, sizing us up—before it slid
Beneath the surface not breaking the surface.

Rarely, rarely it will freeze on the water's edge
And let us watch as long as we remain
Within ourselves—unlike ourselves—barely
Breathing before the small ugly god overlooking
The world it brought our senses to.

The Body Smells

No wonder dogs love us, they who love to smell.
We must be music to their noses,
An orchestra of odors—tang of armpits,
Morning breath, earwax wafting
Via Q-tip and fingertip; feet freed from socks
Locked in shoes all day; genitals mummified
Every morning, unwrapped, unleashed each night;
All our internal functions and fluids—asparagus
Scent of urine, periodic table of blood, tears, shit, vomit,
Weeping wounds; the low comedy of farts.
Our essential selves slipping out—
Brine and oil oozing from our pores into the famous
Smell of fear. Hope's chemistry rising
From us like warm bread.
And the whiff we are always chasing, sweetness
Elusive as déjà vu on the tip of our tongues,
A whistle too high for us to hear that dogs
Absorb in their sleep, their wet nostrils flooded
With the truffle-deep, loamy aroma of love.

Good Dog

When I walk the dog I let the dog
Decide where we go. I keep the leash loose
And follow in her footsteps to the busy street
That scares us both, but it's the only way
To the grand tree at the corner where she stands
In a trance, her nose vacuuming the bulging roots
For a snoot-full of who-knows-what.

Or she heads the other way, to the empty lot,
A minefield of turds I step through gingerly
While she throws herself on the foulest ones
And spins like a washing machine,
Then trots to the puddle by the curb and takes
A long drink, lapping it up like champagne,
Splashing as if it were the fountain of puppyhood.

Her shanks and feathers drenched,
She looks at me as if I envy her
And seems to say *okay, I'm good*
And wet and camouflaged in the scent of excrement,
Let's go home and I'll slip beneath your desk
Into a dream of running squirrels into trees
While you take the heat for letting me get into everything.

The Rose Bus

Every Valentine's Day it appears—
Rounded as a loaf of bread, chromed
As a toaster—parked in a frozen, hard-
Scrabble lot beneath a sign for a motel
That isn't Just Ahead anymore.

Rows of vases holding roses
Fill the luggage bays
And behind the windshield
Smaller vases line the dash,
Each one holding a single rose
Rising out of baby's breath.

Someone is in the driver's seat—
Engine running, the bus warm
As a greenhouse—someone
Waiting to push open the door,
Let enter love's latest customers.

I Love Chickens

Because they spend the day paying attention—
One eye looking for what they can eat,

One for what can eat them. Because they hang with me
In the yard, their clucks and coos a comfort

While I plant and they dig. Because for them
Roaches are a rare and challenging treat.

Because an egg tucked amid pine shavings in the dark
Coop is a brightness and a marvel. Every day.

Because their eggs are not only white but also brown,
And blue, and dappled, and fit perfectly into my palm.

Because they walk like wind-up toys and run
Akilter, careening like roller-coaster cars.

Because everything we haven't eaten tastes like them.
Because they are delicious. And their eggs are delicious.

Because they are a world of recipes: Cordon Bleu,
Kiev, Curry, Florentine, Parmigiana, Pot-pie.

Because each of the one-hundred folds in a chef's hat
Represents a different way to cook an egg.

Because sometimes they think I am a rooster
And squat down to be mounted.

Because they are not mascots for sports teams
Even though they are fierce with their hypodermic

Beaks and their scaly feet's claws.
Because they like to have their scaly feet rubbed.

Because after eating they use the grass like a napkin
To wipe their beaks. Because they are flappable.

Because every night they return to their coop
And every morning they walk the plank into their day.

Because like us they brood, follow a pecking order, desire
A nest egg. Because even their shit is useful.

Only Itself

Nothing depends on it, the rust encrusted
Wheelbarrow turned on its side, the tray
Eaten through, one handgrip missing, the other
Split, the tire cracked and vine-wrapped.

Someone has ringed it with bricks and left it
In the center of the turnaround at the alley's end,
Where only the trash truck and the lost go. It looks
Like a sun dial without a shadow, like landing gear

Without wings. No, it looks only like itself—worn out
Hauler of topsoil, manure, mulch, clippings,
Sand and bricks, maybe the same bricks that now
Surround it—this there-and-back heavy lifter,

There-and-back until it ended here, atilt, next to nothing.

Gun on the Table

My favorite scene in *Body Heat* has nothing
To do with the intricate plot
That William Hurt and Kathleen Turner
Devise to kill her rich, oppressive husband.
My favorite scene, maybe ten seconds long,
Shows Hurt getting into his car as an antique
Roadster drives by, a fully costumed clown
At the wheel, waving. Hurt stares, slightly
Bewildered, while the clown passes and disappears.
That's it. Cut to Hurt and Turner in another
Sweaty sex scene and post-coital planning,
The foregone noir conclusion closing in. Meanwhile,
Since we know there are no meaningless details
In art, we keep expecting the clown to reappear
Or at least figure indirectly in the action.
Like Chekhov said—if there's a gun on the table
In act one, it had better be fired by act three.
But no, the clown is random, there and gone, an odd,
Unrelated moment like any of the ones that pass us
Every day and we barely notice
Because life isn't art, isn't revised for coherence,
Not until our lives collapse around us
Like a circus tent in flames
And we begin to look for the alarm we missed.

Wisteria

The way wisteria coils around anything—
Shrubs, hedges, trees, electrical lines—
And dangles its petals like clusters of grapes,

It's hard to keep it from smothering
What holds it without damaging what holds it.
Why cut it back anyway, its fragrance so alluring

Even the dog lifts his head for a better whiff?
The petals fall, the sweetness ends,
But the vine keeps strangling and lengthening,

Just as someone you loved, beautiful and intoxicating,
Wrapped around your life, and the only way to save
Yourself was to cut away the best part of your heart.

Old Glasses

Looking for something, I forget what,
I opened the drop-front desk and found
Inside a cubbyhole an old pair of glasses,
Mine, lenses down, stems folded like arms
Across a chest, skeleton in a casket.

The chipped, clunky frames
And round glass made me think museum,
Model-T, dodo bird, myself when I was still
Becoming me, all confidence and bluff, corner
Of wasn't looking and didn't know, edge
Between blink and shiner.

Off with the new, I tried the old and saw at once
How mild their correction, grandmother's
Light touch bending to adjust my view.
I saw how much nearer to blur and shadows
My true sight had grown, how much detail gone.

I took those glasses off, placed them back
Into their hole and shut the desk.

The Gun Show

Three large meeting rooms of a hotel at an I-95 exit—
Grab a bite, a bathroom break, a gun—you're good to go.
Enough Nazi memorabilia and decoration to make
Ordinary the arsenal of firearms and other
Weaponry—slapjacks, batons, ninja stars, knives
Large and small, hatchets, cleavers, machetes, mace,
Paper weights that might be mistaken for brass knuckles
But everyone knows knucks are illegal.
Tables, tables, tables stacked with bullets, bullets, bullets.
Much of one room is makeshift bookstore—
War books, encyclopedias of guns, bios of assassins
And memoirs by Karl Rove and ilk. Also a story collection
By Eudora Welty and *The Women's Room* by Marilyn French.
From speakers beneath a table a soundtrack—
"Snowbird" and other jaunty tunes from earlier times.
I pick up a machete thinking I could use it to tear
Through smilax and wisteria. Slice my thumb, little faucet
Of blood dripping into my palm. I palm it when the
      dealer starts
Telling me about his Uzi, how it collapses into a pistol.
Good for the back porch, he says, *squirrels and birds.*
      Rabbits too.
My palm is a warm puddle of blood.
The dealer pushes the Uzi toward me, goes on talking
About how you've got to pick up the guns,
Feel them, that's what shows are for.
Everybody is helpful. Please and thank-you, excuse me,
Have a good day, a blessed day, a second amendment day.
With this much firepower within reach, it's wise to be polite.
I thank the Uzi man, conceal my cup of blood running over
And look for an exit or a bathroom, whichever comes first.

Poets

Well before Wallace Stevens,
Sam Colt—poet of steel and wood
According to his lawyer—
Made Hartford, Connecticut, famous,
His armory churning out pistols
Because, as Sam wrote,
"The good people of the world
Are very far from being satisfied
With each other and my arms
Are the best peacemakers."
The Colonel—as he preferred
To be called even though he
Never served—is known for inventing
The revolving cylinder, making it
Possible to shoot six bullets in rapid
Succession without reloading,
A devastating act of imagination.
Others were already working
On the revolver concept
But his lawyer claimed that Sam
Conceived and built his model
Unaware of others' plans.
The lawyer was convincing, the steel
And wood poet got the patent.
Like Eliot said, good poets borrow,
Great poets steal. Sam's genius was more
For gun selling than for gun making.
He was the first to use mass-marketing,
And he commissioned artists
Such as George Catlin to paint scenes
In which a Colt firearm figured prominently.

Too, he was lucky—the Civil War began
Just as his armory reached full production
And his steel and wood poem was chosen
As the sidearm of the Union Army.
Like other famous poets we know, Sam
Was a cheat, a backstabber, a liar, a windbag.
His wife, Elizabeth, however, was as sweet
And genteel as Sam was not. A minister's daughter,
She was a poet, too. Secretly. Until
Sam died in 1862, before he saw the full effect
His poetry had on the world, and Elizabeth
Steered the company to epic size and profit.
She contributed vastly—money, buildings, causes—
To the cultural, artistic, and spiritual life of Hartford,
Where she died in 1905, ten years before
The young lawyer Wallace Stevens arrived
And started walking to and from his job
At the life insurance company secretly
Composing poems in his head.
Sam, Elizabeth, Wallace—all three
Are buried in Hartford's Cedar Hill Cemetery—
But their poetry lives on.

Women and Guns

In the long line to the gun show, more women
And kids than you might guess.
But why not—soon enough I'm looking
At child-size rifles in neon colors
And pink hand guns for the ladies
That fit perfectly into a purse.
And why not—Gun comes from the name of
An enormous weapon in the 14th century,
Domina Gunild, which probably derived
From the Norse female name Gunnhildr.
Whatever, by the 15th century gunne
Was the word for any hand-held firearm,
And there were already a lot of them
Because gun making was a Dark Art,
The sulphur of gunpowder an obvious sign
Of witchcraft, and we know the world—
Both old and new—was full of witches.

The Move

Our friends said we'd be back—or one
Of us would—from mountains' blue views,

Rocks instead of monuments.
Fireflies instead of taillights.

What upheavals it takes—fractures, quakes,
Eruptions—to make mountains, so self-contained

They create their own weather.
In the sky, hawks instead of pigeons.

On the coldest, whitest height we hike
Fearing nothing, not even love.

Beneath our feet, arrowheads
Instead of needles.

The iced lake mirrors us, the slow
Melt at the edges, trees ticking instead of clocks.

The Wages of Mountains

We laid down our bills and imbalances
For mountains, wildflowers loud

In green pastures. We wake to
The gargle of rivers, work to the whistle

Of cardinals. Clouds empty their pockets
At our feet. Stretched half in grass and half

In dust, the black snake speaks in tongues,
Unsaving its skin. We scratch our itch

On bark, hunt honey—our sweetest selves.
Pitched in dew, the spider's tent

Is our revival. We lie down with the moon
Floating up, the tallest bank not tall enough

To touch that loose balloon.

Egrets

Are the last to flee a storm.
The darker and windier
It gets, the louder the thunder,
The calmer they become, standing
Motionless in the marsh.

When it seems the wind must be
Too much for their wings,
They set sail, growing whiter
As they rise against the black wall—
Whiter and smaller.

Inside Georgia

1.

We came in our northern clothes—great coats and long-
    johns,
Boots, gloves, scarves, hats, flaps, flannels—prepared for
    nothing
But winter. But winter isn't winter here, it's alleged
    winter, a-k-a
A breeze, a walk in the park, a picnic, a piece of cake,
    cherry on top.
Last seen in the blooming camellias, unarmed. Our coats
    hang
In the attic like disguises. The red sled hauls bags of
    mulch.
The snow shovel scoops pecans.

2.

The first stir of spring—still sluggish snakes twisted,
    flattened
On shoulders, on blacktop. Sudden flowers like all night
    stars
Fell instead of rain. What Eden was if Eden was.
    Controlled
Burns, woods and fields blackened, ashed. The black
    snake flashing,
A whip across the back of the glass-black lake so thick
    with cypresses
A canoe cannot maneuver, follow herons to their rookery
In the crowns of the most remote trees.

3.

Gnats in infinite swirl. Summer infinite. Brittle grass
    cracking
Like little bones. Heat as cleanser, refiner—ripe dog shit
    dried,
Bleached, seared to powder before our eyes. Clouds rise
Like bread, like water boils into foam. Steam. No rain.
Or else tantrum–wind, thunderbolt, scar of lightning.
    Rain
So furious it bounces, runs, gutters, backs up, floods.
No escape.

4.

Pecans flood. Two trees pour so many we can't manage.
Not us, not the squirrels. All of us, even the dogs, stand
    inside
The drip-line splashing in them, cracking them, digging
The sweet meat, filling ourselves, filling bags, the
    squirrels
Skittering-stashing them in beds, in bike baskets, in gaps
Between bricks, the house shimmed, fortified with
    pecans
The squirrels will never need or remember.

5.

In the fallow field, fire. Tree stumps smoldering in rain,
    afternoon
Charcoal-colored—clouds, breath, smoke, mist. Gunfire
In the woods. Dogs and barking and hunters emerging
    slowly,

Standing out in their camouflage, rifles carried tenderly,
    birds
Carried by the neck—the end of the day's waiting and
    moving,
Silence and rustle, pointing and sighting, squeezing.
Carrying home.

The Lowcountry

In our middle age, our parents
Dead and haunting us
As we become more like them,

We live where we couldn't imagine,
The air so wet-heavy and heated
We can barely breathe on land

That was the bottom of a shallow sea
Epochs ago and is still less
Land than water, more trembling earth

Than solid ground, where fortunes grew
In rice and indigo and malaria
Flowed from rivers to families

And nearly the entire city of Savannah,
Its cemeteries so scenic with the dead
They've turned into parks.

It's hard to live here, to hold
Firm where nothing holds still,
Where deep roots are impossible

And much we once knew can't live.
Yet much that grows nowhere else
Grows in this steamy incubator

Where a wild tree thrives
That some call a come tree
For its heavy smell of sex in spring.

The Next Big Thing

We're at the nursery looking
For something that likes shade,
Grows fast and tall
Enough to fill the space where
Our favorite camellia died,
Leaving a view
Into our neighbor's kitchen.
In the car Stephanie said
She wasn't afraid of dying
When she was younger, but now
She is, especially since summer,
Meaning her brother's sudden death.
Walking through the loamy
Odor of the nursery, I say
It's been the opposite for me—
An irrational fear of death
When I was young but now nothing
More than mild curiosity.
She asks why and all I can say is
All my passages are behind me.
Except for one.
The next big thing is death.
I don't mean it to be funny,
But Stephanie starts laughing.
I've been wondering, she says,
About the next big thing.
Now both of us are laughing
Among the magnolias. We push
Our noses into the flowers'
Creamy cups and breathe
Their citrus scent. We take home

A Little Gem and plant it.
We still see our neighbors
Moving around in their kitchen,
But in a few years we will see nothing
But dark green leaves and white
Flowers the size of chalices.

The Fence Line

All day workers
Have been raising a stockade
Fence between my neighbor's yard and mine.
I don't mind—I'm cynical
Enough to think good fences
Make good neighbors.
What rattles me is how terrible
The noise, how battle-like
The intermittent whining saw,
The rapid fire and random
Clank, echo of iron, splintering ricochet.
When it stops at last and everyone
Is gone, I go into the quiet afternoon,
The sun a soft red ball, to view the aftermath.
From end to end the fence
Runs plumb, the look of true
Craft and art—all that chaos hammered into line—
The fresh-cut pine sweetening the air.
And already a mockingbird perching
Repeating what it heard all day.

Feeders

You can have birds.

Hang from an eave a feeder
Filled with seeds,
They will find it—

The little dusty ones first,
Sparrows and wrens and then

Like flames, cardinals
And orioles and warblers,

The cool blue flash of jays
And buntings, yin-yang
Of chickadees.

They'll splash in the seeds
And sing in the shower, spillover
Rooting below.

The air which seemed both
Empty and heavy
Will vibrate with wing-flash and whistle.

In the natural light of the window
Where you reflect, you will feed
Your hunger for wonder.

The Guitars

Waiting for green in a dried-up Georgia
Town at the intersection
Of passing-through and going-nowhere,

I squint through heat waves at eight
Acoustic guitars side by side
Against the wall of a boarded-up Jiffy Lube.

I search for a sign or for someone minding
From the ledge of shade, but there's no one
And nothing except the inexplicable

Guitars lined up and left
To the imagination—their bodies shields
Throwing back the sun's dumb glare.

Around me other drivers shift
Their attention from the traffic signal
To this signal of another kind, strumming

Long after the light turns
And we move forward, slowly
Turning our gazes back to the road.

Fair Road

Sun down but not out,
Houses reduced
To window glow,

Camellias twinkle pink
At the speed of headlights.
In the strip mall more stores

Have closed but one
Like Jesus
Is always coming soon.

It's cold and growing colder,
Still the ball fields are filled
With cheer, bright bats

Thwacked, long flies dropping
Like stars at the warning
Track of whatever joy

Can be run down and gloved,
Breath blasting holes
Through night's blue wall.

Georgia Sunset

How scarred we are, how familiar
With hospitals and humiliation
And the gloved hands of strangers.
Love is everything and everything
Is not enough. The telephone rings
To death and all we can do is answer.

Flying back from your mother's
Funeral in the city where every road
Once led to us, above the knuckled
Mountains where we lived long enough
To always long for them,

Down the coast to the sea level hot-house
That is the only home our children know,
I watch the plane's shadow
Tracking us, hugging the landscape
Across valleys, ridges, clay, swamp.

Landing, I recall taking off
Into a gorgeous setting sun
That never set as we flew towards it,
Westward, time moving backward.

Pendulum

Time, I had you all wrong,
Dwelled too long on your shortcomings—
How you walk in without knocking,
Read the notes on my calendar,
Write notes on my calendar.
You talk too fast and too often. You smother.
But when fire sweeps my heart
Blackening everything, the great trees
Burning all at once like a matchbook,
Cindered all at once,
It's you quietly returning green
One painful shoot at a time,
One needle, one buried seed.
And oh, you make me laugh playing
Tricks on me—Vaseline on my glasses,
Mussing my hair, sucking gas from my tank.
And when you hug me I feel hugged for real,
Breathless. Never mind the gun tucked
Behind your back. I know it's just
For protection.

The Yard in April

We're rolling around, digging dirt.
Not planting, just rolling and digging, rubbing
Elbows with doodle-bugs. Nosing mulch.

A bumble bee's head, snub as a boxing glove,
Jabs and disappears into the soft folds of a rose,
Withdraws and burrows in again, and again.

The ferns roll out their fronds like carpets.
In a week, ten days, the dogwoods' small fists
Will open fully, palms up, dove white.

Beneath the skirt of the loropetalum, we're luckier
Than clover. Only the worms know where we are.
But they know where everyone is.

All around us it's spangles and tassels. Fireworks
Without noise, or darkness.
We stretch out on green and awe our eyes.

The Tenderness of Ice

The comfort of hospitals is ice—
The cold full cup of slivers

For a loved one to rub across
The patient's parched, sealed lips

Before food or water is allowed.
Before the patient is conscious,

The ice is guided back and forth,
The melt dripping from the corners

Of the patient's mouth, and from
The loved one's numbed fingertips

As the lips bloom into color, part slightly
And, saying nothing, ask for more.

Small Wonders

1.

Cars swerve to avoid
An old straw hat
Lying in the street.

2.

Overcast all day—still
The sunflowers inch their great heads
East to west, tracking the sun.

3.

The towering clock
In front of the funeral home
Has stopped running.

4.

The bird-filled woods, felled,
Became the house that never sold—
Grass seed eaten, straw taken for nests.

5.

In the river, the stones
Are round and flat and shine.
On my desk, round and flat.

6.

On the road, dead
Baby birds, dead frogs, dead snakes:
The other signs of spring.

7.

Dogs know what to do
With the dead—
Roll in them.

8.

Why oppose opposites?
A hammer pulls as well as drives.
Only what is buried grows.

9.

With its own harsh tongue
The wounded cat
Heals itself.

10.

On the sun-scorched dog turd
A new butterfly
Spreads its wings.

11.

Bright autumn day—
The room darkens leaf by leaf
Landing on the skylight.

12.

Some trees leaf out top down,
Some bottom up. By summer
Who knows which is which?

13.

A thousand different greens
Make the mountain's
Singular green.

About the Author

Eric Nelson's five previous poetry collections include *The Twins*, winner of the Split Oak Press Chapbook Award; *Terrestrials*, winner of the X.J. Kennedy Poetry Award; and *The Interpretation of Waking Life*, winner of the Arkansas Poetry Award. His poems have appeared in *Poetry*, *The Cincinnati Review*, *Southern Poetry Review*, *The Oxford American*, *The Sun*, and many other venues. He and his wife, the writer Stephanie Tames, live in Asheville, North Carolina.

Poetry from Gival Press

Tickets for a Closing Play by Janet I. Buck
Voyeur by Rich Murphy
We Deserve the Gods We Ask For by Seth Brady Tucker
Where a Poet Ought Not / Où c'qui faut pas by G. Tod
   Slone

For a complete list of Gival Press titles, visit:
www.givalpress.com.

Books available from Follett, your favorite bookstore, on-line booksellers, or directly from Gival Press.

Gival Press, LLC
PO Box 3812
Arlington, VA 22203
givalpress@yahoo.com
703.351.0079